CREDIT
AND
COLLECTIONS

CREDIT AND COLLECTIONS

THE REAL WORLD

JOHN KOVALCHEK

authorHOUSE®

AuthorHouse™
1663 Liberty Drive
Bloomington, IN 47403
www.authorhouse.com
Phone: 1-800-839-8640

Published by AuthorHouse   10/17/2012

ISBN: 978-1-4772-8219-9 (sc)
ISBN: 978-1-4772-8218-2 (e)

Library of Congress Control Number: 2012919597

CONTENTS

INTRODUCTION

Each year numerous articles are written with regard to the credit function and its place in the corporate structure. If there is any agreement at all among the educators and practitioners, it is that no one set course of education or career path has yet been established for individuals who wish to pursue a career in credit administration.

One credit manager says that, once in credit management, he can't imagine performing without motivation to obtain accounting knowledge while another manager believes being an accountant is a detriment to being a good credit manager. Accounting deals in numbers; credit managers deal with people.

A vice president of a large corporation says that he would rather convert a sharp sales person into a credit manager than try to convert a sharp accountant. Yet, another feels that while a broad background is an asset; financial training is a necessity.

A general consensus is that the credit manager in any organization is a recognized generalist. The credit manager must maximize profitable sales and keep losses to a minimum. Credit management must know accounting, manufacturing, marketing and public relations as well as being well-versed in general business conditions and company objectives in order to assess the risk in daily decisions.

A curriculum at this time in credit administration is not offered toward a degree. Most clerks, managers and credit executives now applying their skills to the trade have learned from trial and error or, at best, from the many informative articles and seminars provided by the profession.

This book is intended to be used as a guide for the small and medium size companies who do not presently have a formal credit and collection program. It is also for those who have implemented an informal program but now have a need to place re-emphasis on the most important phase of their business.

With the economy in its rapidly fluctuating peaks and valleys and tight money supplies management must be made aware of the serious need to review their credit administration. The information contained herein should assist all management in reviewing their current credit functions and responsibilities in order to effect required changes.

THE CREDIT FUNCTION

As a practical matter, the credit function is created for each company, partnership or proprietorship as a sale of merchandise or services is made on other than a cash basis. In fact, terms of sale are offered any time the seller agrees to wait for payment of goods. This could be one hour, one day or 30 days depending upon the "terms" allowed by the supplier.

The corner grocer, by allowing a customer to take merchandise for payment next week and entering the purchase in his "receivables record" has offered credit terms just as much as the giant corporation who concludes a $100,000 sale, issues invoicing and enters the sale in their accounts receivable records. In each case, the basic accountability for the transaction is the same in the credit sale. The corporation employs lawyers, controllers and credit managers to be at their disposal if the large amount is not paid within prescribed terms; the grocer has the customer's word and honor to depend upon. In either example, non-payment will result in elimination of any future business with the customer, and each operating entity stands to lose income from the bad debt.

In this text, the major concentration is the commercial enterprise who anticipates or has established terms for sale of merchandise or services to another commercial entity.

The credit function is as simple or as complex as there are the number and sizes of businesses who recognize the importance of the function and desire to manage it correctly. Credit can be administered by the owner or family member in a closely held company to a credit executive and large staff in a major corporation. In either case, the problems are similar in granting credit; the resources to solve the problems vary with the size of company and method of operation.

In many companies the controller, accountant or office manager may be assigned the responsibility for the credit function. He or she may have little or no authority to approve or disapprove an order but is directed to collect for the sale within a specified period of time. Those who have credit staffs and managers are usually given authority for control of the customer's accounts from initial acceptance of an order through the actual collection.

Whichever method of assigning duties is used for the credit function, there are basic objectives that must be achieved in order to assure the efficient management of cash flow and to minimize the risk exposure for one of the major liquid assets of the business.

A. CREDIT POLICIES AND PROCEDURES

Before any attempt is made to newly create or change the credit function, management must develop the policies and procedures by which credit administration is expected to operate within the organization. The policies and procedures should be as clear and concise as possible to avoid later conflicts with sales and customers. Extreme care should be exercised to assure that the credit function can operate within the guidelines to be approved by management.

Once the policies and procedures are formally written, they must be accepted and approved by the management. Only in this way will the credit administrator be able to exercise the decision-making processes needed to maximize profits. The lack of formal policies and procedures will eventually lead to confusion with the customers, conflicts with sales personnel and administrative inconsistencies that could result in the loss of business or even legal problems

Following is a suggested procedure that may be used to meet individual requirements.

Date Effective:

SUBJECT: CREDIT/COLLECTION PROCEDURE

PURPOSE: To define responsibilities of personnel and outline functional routines for maintaining Credit/Collection Department operations and control detail.

PROCEDURE: *Accounts Receivable*

I. *New Account Approval*

    A. *Sales Department* - Potential new accounts are submitted to headquarters—Assistant Sales Manager, on a New Account Credit Application (See Exhibit I). The credit application is processed as follows:

        1. The Assistant Sales Manager shall check data submitted on the form for completeness and accuracy.

        2. Once the Sales Department obtains complete data, the form is transferred to the Credit Department for credit checks, et cetera, (see I, B & C).

        3. After credit approval and assignment of line of credit, the form is returned to Sales.

        4. The Sales Department shall be responsible, with Data Processing, for assigning the proper salesman and customer number after approval on the credit application by the necessary Sales management.

        5. Upon completion of the above requirements, the credit application will be returned to the Credit Department for placement in the permanent credit files.

B. *Credit Department* - As potential new account credit applications are received in the Credit Department, a credit investigation is immediately initiated to determine whether credit terms should be extended to the candidate and to what limits. Sources used to make these determinations are:

1. Financial statements (if available) are analyzed to determine worth and credit limits.

2. Dun & Bradstreet report is ordered.

3. Credit references (at least three) are called to obtain necessary information.

4. Bank reference(s) are called or contacted in writing to obtain complete financial data.

C. *Credit Determinations* - The credit investigations will determine if the account is a risk or credit-worthy customer.

1. Credit-worthy accounts will be further analyzed to establish reasonable lines of credit. The Credit Manager and/or Assistant Manager will recommend credit limits for approval by the Director of Credits and Collections.

2. Risk account determinations will be reported to the Sales Department and the customer is notified that payment by certified check is required in advance of order entry.

II. **Existing Accounts**

A. *Order Processing - All Locations* - All orders received from customers who are current, have no balance, and are less than the established line of credit, may be processed through the order entry system immediately after reviewing them against the A/R Past Due Listing. Credit for accounts that are past due must be sent to the Credit Department if received at Headquarters. Those received at other locations in the past due status will be referred to the Headquarters Credit Department by telephone.

The following determinations are considered in approving or disproving an order:

1. The account's present status is analyzed for current or past due balances.

    a. If an account is current, the payment history is considered, as well as potential default on the order value.

    b. If an account is 1 to 30 days past net due date, the order may be held and the account contacted by phone to advise them of their status. The order will be held until satisfactory arrangements are made to reconcile the past due amounts. A confirming form letter will be mailed following the phone conversation (to customer and sales).

    c. The open order file will be reviewed to determine the status and value of orders in process. The amount open will be considered in approving the current order within established line of credit.

2. Orders received on zero balance accounts will have:

    a. Past payment history analyzed for payment frequency.

    b. Updated credit report will be ordered for accounts inactive over six months.

3. If it becomes necessary to change or withdraw the credit status for an order in the open order file, the Credit Department will pull the shipping copies to stop shipment. On special orders millwork, production copies will be pulled. The customer will then be contacted and alternate financial arrangements negotiated before the shipment is released.

III. *Collection of Accounts*

A. *Discount Terms* - Sales are made under the following terms and conditions:

1. Product A (or Division) 2% ADF 10th prox, net EOM prox. (except direct shipments of truck or carloads) . . . . 2% ADF 5 days after arrival.

2. Product B (or Division) 2% 10th prox. Net EOM prox. (except on certain direct future shipments) . . . . Net 10th prox.

3. Product C (or Division) Net 30 days

4. Product D (or Division) 2% 10 days, Net 30

5. Product E (or Division) 2% 10 days, Net 30

B. *Past Due - 1-30 Days* - When a customer falls into this category, a phone call is usually made to determine the reason and/or a follow-up letter (see Exhibit II) is issued.

C. *Past Due - 31-60 Days* - Accounts in this category are issued a letter (see Exhibit III) informing the account of removal of open credit terms unless the balance is brought to a current status. In this instance orders are usually held until the balance is cleared.

D. *Past Due - 61-90 Days* - The account will be telephoned to resolve the past due amount. A confirming letter will be issued on the phone conversation.

E. *Past Due - 91-120 Days* - A pre-collection call and letter (see Exhibit IV) is initiated to inform the account of legal action to be taken. All orders are held and open-account status is immediately discontinued.

In the event a customer in this category fulfills his obligation, he shall continue to remain on a cash-in-advance basis. Open credit terms will only be reinstated after the customer has demonstrated the ability to pay on a current basis. Depending upon the customer and/or size of the order, stand-by letters of credit may be used.

Accounts under $25M and in this category may be referred to a Collection Agency or Attorney. After a 10-day free demand period, the accounts are transferred to a bad debt reserve account. Any funds received from the Collection Agency or Attorney will be credited to the account as a recovery. Accounts in excess of $25M must have written permission from Corporate before processing.

F. *Past Due Reduction Report* - A weekly past due reduction report for those accounts in the 91 and above category is submitted to the Accounting Department by the Credit Manager. These figures are used as a part of the status report to management.

IV. *Late Payment Service Charge*

A. *Rate* - All shipments will bear interest at the maximum rate or fraction thereof, as allowed by law, immediately following net due date of invoice.

B. *Application of Charges* - The Credit Manager shall review accounts appearing on the monthly past due listing to prepare the interest charges to be levied.

The Credit Department will indicate those customers to receive interest charges and forward the information to Data Processing. Service charge invoices will be prepared and mailed to the customers.

EXHIBIT I

NEW ACCOUNT APPLICATION

New_____ Change _____ Delete _____   Date _____

SALESMAN _____

Business Name _____   Telephone No. _____   County _____

Account No. _____ Address _____   City _____ State _____ Zip _____

Cust. Showroom Address _____   Approx. Sq. Ft. _____

Warehouse Address _____   Approx. Sq. Ft. _____

PERSONNEL AND SALES DATA   PRODUCT LINES AUTHORIZED TO PURCHASE

President _____   ☐ Product A

Vice President _____   ☐ Product B

Treasurer _____   ☐ Product C

Sales Manager _____   ☐ Product D

Number of Employees _____   ☐ Product E

Approximate Yearly Sales _____   ☐ Other

Potential Annual Purchases from M W _____

Is this a potential stocking customer _____   Is this customer a major distributor in this area _____

TYPE OF ORGANIZATION   TYPE OF BUSINESS: ☐ Retail Building Material Dealer   ☐ Retail Hardware Store

☐ Corporation   ☐ Partnership   ☐ Wholesale Distributor   ☐ Concrete Company   ☐ Home Manufacturer

☐ Individually Owned   ☐ Drywall Company   Other _____

CREDIT DATA

D & B Rating _____ Net Worth _____

Customer's Bank _____   Bank Official _____   Phone No. _____

Three References   1. _____
(Name, Complete   NAME   PHONE NO.
Address & Phone No.)
                      _____
                       ADDRESS   CITY   STATE   ZIP

                   2. _____
                       NAME   PHONE NO.

                      _____
                       ADDRESS   CITY   STATE   ZIP

                   3. _____
                       NAME   PHONE NO.

                      _____
                       ADDRESS   CITY   STATE   ZIP

Is this customer's Financial Statement attached _____ If No Give Reason _____

Sales Tax Exemption Certificate No. _____ State _____ (Attach copy of certificate)

ATTEST: This Application and Financial Statement is true and correct as of _____, 19____, and given by applicant in order to induce
the extension of credit to the applicant and guarantors. By executing this credit application, I/We recognize and agree to the terms and
conditions as shown on the invoicing of ____Manufacturers. By acceptance of this application, we grant____ the right to retrieve all
property itemized on any unpaid invoices.

            PRINCIPAL/OWNER _____

MARKETING APPROVAL:		CREDIT APPROVAL:	
APPROVED _____	DATE _____	APPROVED _____	DATE _____
REJECTED _____	DATE _____	REJECTED _____	DATE _____
Returned to Salesman by _____		LINE OF CREDIT _____	

EXHIBIT II

Date

Customer Name
Address

Re: Your Account No.

Gentlemen:

We are sorry to note that your account includes past due items totaling
$. We certainly hope that your check is on the way. If not, your
remittance by return mail can still reach us ahead of our monthly closing
on (date).

Please consider your (current month) account in the amount of $ which
will also become past due on that date. You can avoid a service charge by
including this.

Your cooperation is greatly appreciated.

Sincerely,

MANUFACTURERS

EXHIBIT III

Date

Customer Name
Address

Re: Your Account No.

Gentlemen:

When reviewing our statement of your account, we are concerned to note that it has become delinquent. The following summary indicates that we have not received payment for certain invoices within the previous months:

(month) Invoices $
(month) Invoices
Other _____
Total Past Due $

We have certainly tried to meet your requirements for building materials and related items and trust that we have been able to do so to your satisfaction.

In order to honor your orders and avoid additional service charges, we must request that your remittance for this portion of your account be received by (date).

Yours very truly,

MANUFACTURERS

EXHIBIT IV

Date

Customer Name
Address

Re: Your Account No.

Gentlemen:

We have become increasingly concerned to note that items within our statement of your account have not been paid.

(month) Invoices	$
(month) Invoices	
(month) Invoices	_____
	$_____

In addition to incurring service charges, there is also the fact that we are frequently asked to share our credit experience with other companies or credit bureaus.

We strongly urge that the payment of the past due portion of your account reach our office by (date) so that we may avoid taking other measures.

Yours truly,

MANUFACTURERS

B. SETTING CREDIT GOALS

The credit administrator and upper management should set certain goals by which the credit function will be measured. The following goals are easily determinable and should be developed for reporting to management on a monthly basis.

1. *Accounts Receivable Turnover Goal*

The receivables turnover rate is a ratio that tests the quality of receivables. The turnover of receivables is calculated as follows:

Receivables Turnover = Annual Net Sales/Accounts Receivable

It has always been difficult for one to relate a turnover rate of 8.33 times to anything concrete; however, credit people can relate days outstanding to collection periods or terms offered.

The collection period in days can more easily be calculated by the following formula;

Collection period (days) = Accounts Receivable x 360/Net Sales

Under this example, a period of 30 days can be more easily related to terms offered. In order to calculate a monthly collection period and to provide a reasonable allowance for monthly variables resulting from shifts in receivable balances due to large or short payments and fluctuations in monthly sales volumes, the recommended procedure is to use the average of three months sales divided into the average ending receivables. The collection period is then related to an agreed standard set by management or taken from trade journals or financial statistics provided by sources such as Dun & Bradstreet.

Once the collection period goal has been established, it is the responsibility of credit management to administer programs in order to meet or exceed that goal. The methods by which this can be accomplished will be explained in detail in the following chapters.

The main point here is to determine if the collection period calculated is reasonable for the company. Normally the collection period should not e excessive when comparing it to the selling terms being offered. For example, it would be excessive if a company's terms were not 10 days and the collection period was calculated to be 30 days. This could indicate some slowness in collection of receivables. The same 30 days might be acceptable however, if the selling terms were set at 30 days or longer.

2. *Limiting Bad Debts*

The goal for allowable bad debts is mostly determined by the management. Industry guidelines are available, but the final decision rests with management's ability to withstand loses of allowable amounts. Where there are no bad debts, the company is either on a cash basis or its receivables are dotted throughout with past due amounts. Depending on the volume of past dues in the receivables, the collection period will rarely decline and perhaps continue to rise.

Most companies will accrue some figure monthly to offset the effect of bad debt write offs. This figure could be some predetermined amount that may be acceptable over a twelve month period or it may be a formula applied against each month's sales based on past debt experience.

One true and most obvious way of determining potential bad debt is to age the accounts receivable. The aging of receivables does not take discount period into consideration since the concern of major importance is related to amounts past net terms due and for what period of time. With a knowledge of selling terms of the company, it is readily discernable as to the past due amounts for each customer. As a past due amount ages out further and further the potential for a bad debt increases and immediate action would be necessary.

3. *Minimizing Disallowed Orders*

One of the most important, and sometimes under stressed functions of credit administration is the approval or disapproval of incoming orders. It is only with the required tools to make sound credit decisions that a credit manager can approve or disapprove an order.

As orders are received daily the credit manager must make a decision on each one which calls for a thorough knowledge of each account. Numerous factors must be weighed and readily available for these decisions. Facts or data such as:

credit line
past dueness
exposure
back-log (open orders)
performance history
financial strength
payment history
industry trend
seasonal peaks
cyclical trends, etc.

must be considered for order approval. Where several or sometimes even one of these facts are in violation the order can be detained or, at worst, lost as a sale forever.

This possible loss of revenue is one of the most critical reasons why the credit function has to be prepared to make daily decisions on each customer. Untimely or complete lack of the necessary data will delay orders and cause the possible loss of a sale or, even worse, that particular customer for good.

As an example, if the customer's account is not updated daily for cash payments or adjustments, the credit manager may be reading an outdated balance which may indicate excessive exposure. The order may be held; the customer will be called and the result would be an irate customer who will cancel the order and may sever business relations permanently.

No customer who paid his balance due likes to be dunned because of the lack of good business sense on the part of his supplier. This area of credit administration is extremely sensitive since misinformation can lead to customer mistrust and a general feeling of incompetency with the supplier.

III

TERMS OF SALE

The offering of credit is a privilege for the buyer and not, as some like to believe, an obligation to the seller. As long as credit is offered in the normal course of business, management will have to contend with the marginal account.

A marginal account, as defined under the limited capital meaning, is one who does not always have the necessary funds to pay for purchases of product within the published terms. The goal of a good credit administrator is to control the number of marginal accounts that are maintained in accounts receivable and to restrict excessive credit allowances. Financing of marginal customers through the accounts receivable provides them with a competitive advantage over customers who pay promptly and creates a heavier burden on your company's cash flow.

Management, in planning cash flow, look toward maintenance of published credit terms to provide a reliance on the turnover of money due the company. If cash flow is a true test for sound credit management then the credit terms offered should be reasonably set for maintenance by the credit department.

Credit terms are policy statements to customers on how you expect them to pay back your money. Generally, terms offered to customers should be consistent within the same customer base or product line and should be enforced. If consistent policy application is not maintained, the aging of accounts will become older and older. The more aged a balance becomes in an account; the less profitable the original sale becomes and the more difficult to achieve collection.

An understanding of the various credit terms being offered is very important from the standpoint of administering your own accounts receivables aging and collection. However, it is also important to know your customers terms of sale and how they work to determine some idea of when you can expect to be paid. The customer's cash flow determines your ability to maintain a current accounts receivable status.

A. *Cash Discount vs. Trade Discount*

A cash discount is the deduction that an open credit account customer is allowed to make from the invoiced amount for submitting their payment within a short period from date of invoice as compared to the net payment period. The purpose of this discount is to encourage earlier payment of the invoice for improving cash flow. The reward to the customer is a discount allowance for the use of their money.

Trade discounts are not offered as a reward for faster payment but are intended to allow a deduction because of performance of a function or because of the purchase of large quantities. This discount may be deducted regardless of when the invoice is remitted.

The credit manager must be prepared to disallow any cash discounts that are deducted after the allowable terms. The selling term should be an enforceable policy and, unless there is some dispute on the invoice, should be policed diligently. Otherwise the incentive to pay early is removed and cash flow will suffer.

The terms of cash discounts are largely determined by the norms within the industry in which you trade. Factors such as the length of time in which the customer will hold the goods for processing or resell and the competitive conditions of the industry of the seller are the main bases on which the length of terms may be set.

Regular terms published on the company invoicing or statements and dictated by policy are usually offered to the greater percentage of a company's customers when sold on open credit. Terms that differ in length of time or amount are usually negotiated between the buyer and seller for special circumstances and should be considered as special terms.

These situations should be kept to a minimum since it affects the cost of the sale and the aging of receivables.

Published selling terms should clearly indicate the cash discount percentage, where allowed, the length of time permitted to make the deduction from the gross invoice amount; a trade discount, if included; and the allowable amount of time to when the gross amount of the invoice is due for payment.

B. *Selling Terms*

The following list will serve to illustrate the abbreviations and symbols used when expressing selling terms.

N 30	Net 30 days
2%/10, N 30	2% cash discount within 10 days, gross amount due in 30 days
2% 10th prox, Net Eom Prov	2% cash discount by the 10th of the next following (proximo) month, gross amount due by the next following end of month
2%/30	2% trade discount allowed. The credit terms are 30 days. The trade discount is not affected by late payment.
Net 10 Prox	Since prox. is the abbreviation for proximo or following month the invoice is due the 10th of the month following the invoicing month

With the prime rate as volatile as it has been over the past year, credit management must be aware of discounts being offered and the costs associated to the company. Since competition, industry payment practices and credit worthiness of customers should be considered when setting discounts, management must weigh the costs carefully. For example,

2%/10, net 30 day terms will cost 37% per annum to have cash 20 days sooner than under net 30 day terms.

The formula for computing the cost and the costs of some credit terms are as follows:

Cost = Discount Percent/(100 - Discount Percent X 365/(Final Due Date - Discount Period

Credit Terms	Cost
1%/10, Net 30	18.4%
2%/10, Net 30	37.2%
2% 10th prox, Net 30 Eom (if not received until the 15th)	49.7%
1%/10, Net 60	7.3%
2%/10, Net 60	14.9%

C. *Non-Open Account Terms*

Usually grouped with the non-open account terms are those referred to as "cash" terms. Many believe that when products are sold for cash there is no credit extended. This is not true since goods shipped "cash" are subject to an expressed or implied understanding that the customer has 10 days credit for checking the merchandise and verifying the invoicing. Payment of the invoice is due within 10 days and if not paid, the seller's only recourse is to pursue payment under the same guidelines as open credit terms.

Some of the most restrictive credit terms are CWO (Cash With Order); CIA (Cash in Advance) and CBS (Cash Before Shipment). All of these terms are similar in that the seller requires that the customer send payment in full for the material either before the order is entered into production or at least before the order is shipped. The terms are requested usually from high risk customers.

COD (Cash on Delivery) terms are also offered to high risk buyers. The cash on delivery requirement removes all danger of a credit loss involving the entire amount of the shipment as long as control of the merchandise remains with the shipper until payment is received. The risk involved is that the customer may not have the cash available to pay on arrival and a number of transportation charges are incurred. Additionally, inventory investment costs and reselling expenses may also result.

IV

DEVELOPING CREDIT GUIDELINES

One of the primary aspects of developing a sound customer base is to initiate the assignment of credit lines or credit guides. These are sometimes also referred to as credit limits.

Some preference seems to be given to the terms "credit lines" rather than "credit limits", since there is more flexibility to a guidelines approach than to a limit which tends to infer strict adherence. With the guideline approach management is allowed to monitor the amount and allow some flexibility against the assignment credit guideline.

To initiate credit lines for everyone in the customer base, the credit administrator needs to obtain a number of detailed facts about each customer. Ideally, this information or most of it, should have been made available when developing the new customer account information. Unfortunately, most companies would have been selling to many customers for a period of time long before the concept of credit files or a formal credit department became a major priority.

Whatever size of a company conducts business with a credit sale, the need for credit files and credit lines are of utmost importance. It is up to the seller to control how much he is willing to sell to another company. Selling on open credit at an uncontrolled rate may look good on the books for receivables but it will never be cash in the bank until it is paid. Write-offs of unpaid sales does not create cash; it adds to the cost of doing business.

The additional cost incurred by making unpaid sales is compounded if one considers the loss of effort that could have been expended on a sale to some good credit risk.

The credit file, in its basic concept, has nothing to do with the type or size of accounting functions that exists within the organization. Accounting merely records the transactions that occur pursuant to a credit sale. Accounting does not make the decision to initiate the open account sale, nor does it collect the money after the sale is made. It is the credit and collection function that must make these decisions with whatever tools are necessary to give assistance—thus credit files and credit lines for each customer.

It does not matter if the organization has a high speed computerized system, mini-computer, electronic bookkeeping machines, or a one-write manual system. The credit files, credit guides and ultimate collection of an open account are the pure inter-related actions of the credit function.

A. *Initiating & Maintaining the Credit File*

Even if there is little or nothing initially to place in a credit file, a physical file with folders and storage space must be created. The steps to follow and information to be recorded should be somewhat near to the following checklist:

— create a file folder for each customer that has an open sale on the account or that will be sold on open account in the near future.

— label each file with the basic identification data for instant reference. Minimum data should be:

1. Customer sold-to name and address
2. Customer account number
3. Name of contact at this location
4. Telephone number
5. Space for credit guide if not available at the time

Other data that may be added at the time or on a later date would be tax codes, credit rating, date customer added to file, and customer status code.

— as folders are completed, file them alphabetically by customer name.

— place statements, trade reports, account status correspondence, collection letters and any other data that is pertinent to the open credit account. Some care should be taken to eliminate any paper from the file that is not directly associated with the customer's credit history.

The credit files, at this point, should begin to relate a story about the customer. Paying habits become more obvious as compared to statements, collection letters, notes and other historical data that is now available in one file for review.

Considering the company terms of sale, the credit manager should begin immediately to assign a credit line for each customer. The active accounts are the priority and should be attacked first.

B. *Setting Credit Lines*

There have been many articles published which attempt to establish various criteria for determining credit guides. The basic and very quick way of establishing a credit line is to calculate 10% of net worth. While the approach assumes you are willing to take a risk on the liquidity of 10% of a customers net worth; there may be many more extenuating factors such as loan guarantees after-acquired clauses for inventories, overstated assets, etc., which can numb this approach.

For instance, a company may have a $50,000 net worth which, at 10%, would allow a credit line of $5,000 of exposure. Through a fast turnover of inventories and collection of receivables, this same customer may be able to purchase and pay for three times that much on a discounting basis. On the other hand, how willing would you be to provide a credit line of $75,000 if the customer had a $750,000 net worth, their collections were slow and inventories were high. His net worth may justify the credit guide; however, payments may be slow in coming. If payment is not made, the only way to collect against net worth is to liquidate the assets and no credit manager wants to go through that process.

Another approach is to develop a matrix for suggested lines of credit based on rating services. This concept measures the customer's ability to pay based on the estimated financial strength as reported to the rating service and the composite credit appraisal developed through their history files. A suggested matrix is included; however, it must be remembered that this could be modified for your needs by the other trade ratings or references that may be utilized in your industry.

CREDIT LINE MATRIX

Dun & Bradstreet	*Lumberman's Redbook*	(000) Suggested *Credit Line*
5A1	4A+1	unlimited
4A1	4A1, 3A+1	$200
3A1, 5A2, A1A	3A1, 2A+1, 4A+2	100
2A1, 4A2, B1A	2A1, 1A+1, 3A+2	75
1A1, 3A2, C1A	1A1, 2A+2	60
BA1, 2A2, D1A, A1B	, 1A+2	50
BB1, B1B	1A2	45
CB1, E1A, C1B, A2B	AB1	40
CC1, 1A2, B2B	AB2	35
DC1, BA2, F1A, D1B, C2B	B1	30
BB2, F1B, D2B	B2	25
DD1, CB2, G1A G2B	C1	20
H1A, F1B	C2	18
CC2, J1A	BC1	15
F2B	BC2	12
EE1, DC2, K1A, G1B	D1	10
DD2, H1B, G2B	D2	8
L1A, J1B, H2B	E1	6
FF1, EE2, K1B, J2B	E2	4
FF2, M1A, L1B, K2B	F1, F2	2
GG1, M1B, L2B	EF1, EF2	1
GG2, M2B	G1, G2, others	refer order

There are other more complicated methods of determining credit lines which require the use of electronic data processing. One of the methods used by P.P.&G. is to assign values both positive and negative, to various key ratios derived from the financial statements. Other values are assigned to certain facts such as percent of volume purchased from the company, pay habits, years in business, pre-tax profit (loss) margin, etc. A simplified example is illustrated as follows:

1) Every credit line begins with a customer's tangible net worth. A usual starting point is 10% tangible net worth and the other variables are analyzed to either contribute or reduce the basic credit guide.

     —10% of 100,000 = $10,000 credit guide

2) The next variable may be based upon the percentage of cost of goods furnished to the customer by the company.

Cost of Goods Furnished	Contribution
under 25%	-0-
25% to 50%	+5% of net worth
????	+ 10% of net worth

3) The paying habit of the customer is assigned certain factors such as:

   1. Discounting
   2. Prompt
   3. Net terms
   4. Slow 1-10
   5. Slow 11-30

The assigned codes may then have weights assigned for application to the customer:

Code	Contribution
1	+ 10% of net worth
2	+5% of net worth
3	-0-

4	-2½ of net worth
5	-5% of net worth

Any factor or weight may be assigned to any number of codes which can be determined by credit management. Analysis of the effect of these factors may also require that adjustments be allowed by credit management for inside knowledge of the customer in question that may not have been taken into consideration by the reporting sources.

4) Again, weights can be assigned for years in business as follows:

No of years	*Contribution*
Under 3	*-0-*
3 to 10	+2½ % of net worth
11 and over	+5% of net worth

5) If the profit margin is available, a rate may be applied to each one percent of margin or loss. In this example 2/10 percent of net worth is assigned for each 1% of pre-tax profit margin. As an example, a profit margin of 4.2 percent contributes .84 percent of net worth to the credit line.

6) In analyzing the financial statements, the current ratio (current assets divided by current liabilities) is determined and weighed as follows:

Current ratio	*Contribution*
2.00 and over	+10% of net worth
1.25 to 1.99	+5% of net worth
.75 to 1.24	-0-
Less than .75	-5% of net worth

7) The Liquid or Quick Ratio calculated by dividing the liquid assets (all current assets except inventories) by the current liabilities. The ratio that results may be rated as follows:

Quick Ratio	*Contribution*
2.00 and over	+15% of net worth
1.00 to 1.99	+10% of net worth
.80 to .99	+5% of net worth
.50 to .79	-0-
Less than .50	-5% of net worth

8) Calculation of the ratio of current liabilities to inventory, which determines the relationship of trade payables to inventory, is weighed as follows:

Ratio	*Contribution*
Less than .65	+10% of net worth
.65 to .99	-0-
1.00 and over	-5% of net worth

9) A ratio of inventory to net working capital (current assets less current liabilities measures the adequacy of working capital to support on-hand inventory. Weights may be assigned as follows:

Ratio	*Contribution*
.50 to .99	+5% of net worth
.25 to .49	-0-
Less than .25 or more than .99	-5% of net worth

10) The total of tangible net worth (assets exclude goodwill minus liabilities) and subordinated debt divided by all unsubordinated debt provides a ratio to determine the customer's investment over his borrowing weights may be assigned as follows:

Ratio	*Contribution*
2.00 and over	+10% of net worth
1.00 to 1.99	+5% of net worth
Less than 1.00	-5% of net worth

11) Days sales outstanding (DSO) is calculated by dividing the customer's net receivables by the average daily sales. One can determine that the maximum DSO should be 30 days plus selling terms as a base against which the calculated DSO should be measured. A weight of .10 percent of net worth can be given for each day the ?? allowable DSO exceeds the calculated amount. For example maximum allowable DSO is 45 days; the calculation results in 36 days or 9 days difference. Multiplying .10 percent times 9 days gives .90 percent of net worth or $900 contribution to the credit line. A "o" is assigned where no information is given.

12) The ratio to measure the rate of the turnover of inventory is calculated by dividing cost of goods sold by ending inventory. An excessively high or low turnover rate is considered to be questionable and weights may be assigned as follows:

Radio	*Contribution*
10.00 to 30.00	+10% of net worth
5.00 to 9.99	+5% of net worth
Less than 5.00 or more than 30.0	-0-

A "o" is assigned if no information is submitted by the customer.

A credit limit statement can then be computer generation, using the above ratios, to show

P.O.&G: A concern for the future, credit limits established by formula and computer.

all contributions (positive and negative) which, when combined, will provide the accumulated credit line. Of course, after all components of the credit guide are determined, it must be remembered that the credit administrator is allowed the option of manually increasing or decreasing the credit line based upon privileged knowledge or experience which cannot be quantified for mathematical purposes.

Finally, a series of key ratio analyses may be prepared to be used in conjunction with previously experienced methods of determining credit lines or they may be used separately as determined by the credit administrated. While this method assumes some skill on the part of the user, the following paragraphs should serve to simplify the selection of key ratios and a format by which comparative data can be studied for the decision making process.

The calculation of ratios is nothing more than the reduction to mathematical terms of the relationship between critical items as reported on financial statements. The ratios in themselves have some minor importance in determining a company's well-being; however, they become more meaningful when compared with published industry standards or other companies in the same line of business. The credit administrator must also be cognizant of the fact that the downward or upward movement of the ratio is much more important than the actual ratio being calculated for the period. The industry standards can be found in Dun's Review periodically which provides the average standard as well as the upper and lower quartiles.

Following is a list of key ratios which are used to establish an understanding of a customers financial strength. These ratios have been selected for their ability to easily distinguish a customer's potential to meet his commitments. In establishing and monitoring an efficient credit function, this criteria is of utmost importance.

By calculating and posting the components of the ratio as well as the result itself on a format presented as Exhibit I, the credit administrator will begin to readily detect certain trends to assist in the decision making process especially in assigning credit lines.

	YEAR I	YEAR II	YEAR III	AVERAGE	COMMENTS
NP / NS - measures operating efficiency (net profit divided by net sales x 100% = %)					
NP / NW - measures rate of return on investment (net profit divided by net worth x 100% = %)					
NS / NW - measures turnover of invested capital (net sales divided by net worth = times)					
WORKING CAPITAL TURNOVER - measures adequacy of working capital to support operations (net sales divided by working capital = times)					
FA / NW - portion of net worth invested in fixed assets (fixed assets divided by net worth x 100% = %)					
TD / NW - relates creditors interest to owners (total debt divided by net worth x 100% = %)					
CD / NW - relationship between current creditors and owners investment (current debt divided by net worth x 100% %)					
CD / WC - availability of working capital to meet current obligations (current debt divided by working capital x 100% = %)					

CURRENT RATIO - ability to meet current debts (current assets divided by cur. liabilities x 100% = %)				
LIQUID RATIO (QUICK) - measures protection to short term creditors in cash (current assets less inventories div. by cur. liabilities)				
COLLECTION PERIOD - guideline for collectability (accounts receivable divided by net sales x 360 = days)				
INVENTORY TURNOVER - measures rate of turnover (cost of goods sold div. by ending inventory = times)				
INV / WC - ability of working capital to support inventory (ending inventory div. by working capital x 100% = %)				
ACCOUNTS PAYABLE RATIO - paying habits (accounts payable div. by purchases x 360 = days)				
SHORT TERM LOANS RATIO - backup for inventory				

Net Profit/Net Sales - This ratio is calculated by dividing after tax profit by the net sales. It measures the efficiency of the operation and, when comparing it to industry trends, will depict the adequate of the earnings against sales.

Net Profit/Net Worth - Divide net profit of the company by net worth. Net worth is determined by subtracting total liabilities from total assets. While this ratio will measure operation efficiency, care must be taken in a heavy debt situation since a favorable earning on net worth may indicate a trading on equity and the heavy debt could become burdensome.

What is most important here is that the analyst must consider the industry factors to assure that the company's ratio is within guidelines.

Net Sales/Net Worth - This factor is calculated by dividing the company's net sales (total sales less returns, allowances and any inter-company transactions) by the net worth. This concept measures the relative turnover of invested capital. A large turnover indicates that the company is overtrading and using vendors credit to finance sales with a limited investment by the owners. This measurement becomes more meaningful when comparing the ratio to industry averages.

Net Sales/Working Capital - The ratio is derived by dividing net sales by working capital (current assets minus current liabilities). The factor is known as "working capital turnover" and is used to measure the adequacy of working capital to support the operations by determining its turnover.

This factor is another measure of whether a company is overtrading, i.e., processing too large a volume for the amount of working capital available. The figure is most meaningful if it is very large or if it is near or beyond the high quartile of industry standards. When the ratio is very large and over-trading is suspect, careful attention should be made to the company's short term financing. This condition would appear on the balance sheet as short term bank loans, advances from associated sources and any other available financing.

Cash Flow Potential - This analysis is not a ratio but is calculated by adding annual depreciation to the earnings. Then by subtracting the current portion of long term debt, the difference measures the ability of a firm to meet annual payback of long term debt without depleting working capital.

Fixed Assets/Net Worth - Divide the company's fixed assets by its net worth. The result is that portion of net worth invested in fixed assets. Usually, the ratio should be lower than 100%. If it exceeds 100%, the usual assumption is that creditor's money is actually being used in financing the investment in fixed assets.

Of course, different industries' fixed asset to net worth ratios vary as much as the industries themselves. The figure that is calculated becomes more useful when comparing it with the particular industry mean or average ratio. In any case, it reveals that portion of net worth invested in the fixed assets which are dollars not available to support current operations.

Total Debt/Net Worth - This ratio, calculate by dividing total debts by net worth, is used as a measurement of creditors protection by indicating the amount of net worth that is absorbed by current and other debt. As the ratio becomes higher, there is less protection available for the trade creditor. It serves as an indication of the relationship between the total creditors interest and the owners investment.

As the percentage nears 100%, the net worth becomes too small to absorb any asset shrinkage.

Current Debt/Net Worth - Current debt divided by net worth indicates the relationship between the creditors' current funds and the owners' investments. The higher the ratio the less there will be available for short term creditors. This should be compared to the industries factors to determine the effectiveness of the net worth and what is considered normal exposure.

Current Debt/Warning Capital - The ratio is calculated by dividing current debt including the current portion of long term debt, by the company's working capital. If the ratio appears too large (nearing 100%) or is high compared to industry averages, the company has inadequate working capital to meet current obligations.

A high percentage is another indicator of over-trading which is potentially one of the more dangerous types of customer. Any sudden drop in market conditions will cause an immediate loss of revenues to pay creditors. The chance of collecting the receivable is further diminished by the fact that the heavy debt is most likely secured by the very current asset on which collection has to be made.

Current Ratio-The most common ratio used is calculated by dividing current assets by current liabilities. This ratio offers a general indication of the ability of the firm to meet its current obligations. A ratio of 2:1 for example means that a company has $2.00 in assets for every $1.00 in liabilities. The larger ratio the better, since current assets are those which become available in normal business transactions to pay the current liabilities. This figure again becomes more meaningful when compared to the industry average since the composition of the current assets themselves can make a tremendous difference in the availability of cash to trade creditors.

Current assets with heavy inventory dollars as its major component is certainly not as attractive as one with more cash or receivables and a small inventory. It must be remembered that payment of current debt is dependent upon the liquidity of current assets.

Liquid (quick) Ratio - This ratio indicates the protection afforded short term creditors in cash or near cash assets. It is calculated by dividing all liquid current assets, exclusive of inventory, by the current liabilities. One can readily see that this ratio becomes more meaningful since only the cash or assets that can be easily converted into cash is used to measure the protection of the short term creditors. Inventories are excluded because of the effort needed to dispose of the asset as well as the difficulty of assessing the true value of the inventory itself.

Collection Period - Accounts receivable turnover is calculated by dividing the annual sales by the accounts receivable balance. A collection period in days is then calculated by dividing 360 days by the accounts receivable turnover.

Another method is to divide the accounts receivable by net sales and multiply the product by 360 days. Either process results in the period of days that sales are outstanding. The ratio offers indications of the collectability of receivables and the effectiveness of the flow of funds.

To determine if the collection period is excessive, one must be aware of the selling terms of the company. If the terms were net 10 days, a 30 day collection period would be excessive. Terms of 2% 10th prox. net 30 end of month with a collection period of 30 days would be considered highly desirable. Of course, a comparison with the industry's average collection period would be most helpful and provide another form of measurement.

Inventory Turnover - Calculation of the ratio is completed by dividing the average inventory into the cost of goods sold and multiplying the result by 360 days. If cost of goods sold is not available the net sales should be used even though the results are not quite as accurate.

Like receivables, the inventory turnover rate is used to determine the condition of the inventories and how fast they are sold. Industry averages should be compared to indicate the normal turnover of inventories and whether the inventories on the balance sheet are within reason in relation to the volume of sales.

Inventory/Working Capital - The ratio obtained by dividing average inventories by working capital is a measurement of the adequacy of working capital to support inventories. It is generally agreed that the ratio should be somewhat less than 100%. If it is near or over 100%, the company may be carrying inventories that are much too large to be supported by the financial resources of the company.

As mentioned previously; with the debt to working capital analysis and others, a company with a high inventory to working capital ratio may be over-trading or the company may have excessive obsolete or slow-moving inventories on hand.

Accounts Payable - The accounts payable turnover, calculated by dividing average accounts payable by the purchases, will provide an indication of the paying habits of the company. A high amount of days outstanding indicates that the firm is not discounting and probably paying beyond the net terms.

Short Term Loans - By dividing the short term notes payable by the purchases, a ratio is developed which measures the financing required to back up trade payables for support of the inventory level. Care should be taken when this figure is excessively high in comparison to industry norms since over trading and obsolete or slow-moving inventory can spell trouble for the short term creditor.

The previously discussed methods, individually or in combination with one another should provide the credit administrator with the necessary quantitative tools to assign a credit guide. Other factors such as length of time in business, paying habits, trade reports, etc., will assist in qualifying the customer and the amount of exposure the credit administrator is willing to gamble.

Whatever method or combination of method is used, the credit manager must make a decision on each customer in the file and assign a credit guide. As sales transactions are accumulated and payments are applied, the manager will begin to see a pattern develop and be able to adjust the credit line accordingly to control the exposure.

V

CUSTOMER MASTER FILE

By definition, a customer master file is a complete and inclusive record of the necessary identifying details for all customers with which business has been or will soon be conducted. The customer master file (CMF) may consist of merely a deck of 5x7 cards or a computer data file which is displayed by means of a lengthy computer print-out or cathode ray rube (CRT) in an on-line system.

Whichever system is available, it is of utmost importance that a customer master file be developed. For the small concern, the file will serve as a handy reference for customers follow-up, phone number, credit rating, credit guide, etc. The larger firms will use the CMF for the same purposes as the smaller manual operations; however, the CMF now becomes a part of the data base often referenced to create acknowledgments of order, invoicing, sales analysis, accounting activity, and customer history which are all required for credit management decision making.

There is basic data that should be included on all customer master files regardless of the company's size or purpose. The following outline will serve to list the recommended data; the purpose for which it will be used; and some precautions to take to avoid future problems. An example of the constant data is found in Exhibit II.

Customer Number - Prior to assigning any number to a customer, careful consideration should be made to the size of your current number of customers and any future growth in your customer base. For example, a company with 200 customers in their present base should not provide for a six digit customer number when four digits would be more than sufficient. Likewise, a company should not limit themselves to four digits when their present customer file contains 7,500 customers.

Whatever number of digits is determined to be the most fitting for a particular company, one very important criteria must be followed. Do not assign any significance to the digits used. The number assigned manually or by computer should remain with that customer for the duration of your business relations and even for a period thereafter.

If the customer number contains digits to designate a salesman, territory, state, type of customer, etc., then when any of these significant factors change, a new customer number must be assigned. The possibility of having one active number and one or more inactive numbers for the same customer will result in mass confusion and encourage errors.

For example, if the multiple numbers must remain open in order to preserve sales data, then orders may be entered to an inactive number or cash misapplied. It is highly recommended that significant digits assigned to specific identifying factors be kept separate from the customer identification number.

Sold to Address and Phone Number - Since this data is sued for billing purposes and, in many instances, shipping also, extreme care should be taken when developing this data. Obviously omissions such as including the post office box number only without a street address will certainly cause shipping delay and added expense.

It is important here to note that many costly problems and even fraud can be avoided if a representative of your company physically visits each customer, especially new applicants to verify their address and facilities. there have been too many cases when orders may be phoned in to a company by a person representing himself as a branch of a going concern and requesting a different ship-to delivery on a rush basis. By the time anyone can follow-up, the merchandise and person are long gone and so is your receivable.

Credit Guide and Credit Rating - The importance of this information in the data base customers master file needs little further explanation. However, one point should be made clear in planning the number of digits to allow for the credit rating. Credit rating services such as Dun & Bradstreet, Lumberman's Redbook, etc., will use different designations when rating companies and, more importantly, a different number of digits for their ratings of estimated financial strength and composit credit appraisals. Therefore a sufficient number of digits must be allowed to accommodate the various sizes of rating designations.

A customer with an estimated financial strength (net worth) of $500,000 is rated by Dun and Bradstreet as a 1A1 with a high credit appraisal. The same customer in another rating service, such as Lumberman's National Red Book Service, would be rated as a 3A+1.

Beside now having the requirement for a fourth digit, the credit administrator or sales personnel can become further confused with the assigned credit ratings if there is no reference to the rating service being used to assign the rating. A 3A1 rated customer, if checked in the Dun and Bradstreet reference manual, will show an estimated financial strength of $1,000,000 to $9,999,999. In Lumberman's Red Book, the same 3A1 rating is assigned a value of $300,000 to $500,000. Therefore, if the possibility exists that more than one rating service will be used, a leading digit to designate the service becomes imperative. The customer with a $500,000 estimated financial strength in Dun and Bradstreet would become a D1A1 and, if rated in Lumberman's the same customer would be shown as a L3A+1.

It would be helpful, when using more than one rating service, to choose a primary service for determination of customers rating and credit guide. If particular customers are then not listed in the primary rating service; the secondary service would be utilized.

The preceding fixed data must be included in all customer master files. Of course, there are many more items that should be included in the master file, but they consist of variable information which require constant updating and maintenance. In a manual system, this chore becomes next to impossible if there are any number of customers being serviced. The following chapter provides most of the requirements needed to either convert to a computerized system or to update existing batch mode on first generation systems.

CUSTOMER MASTER FILE

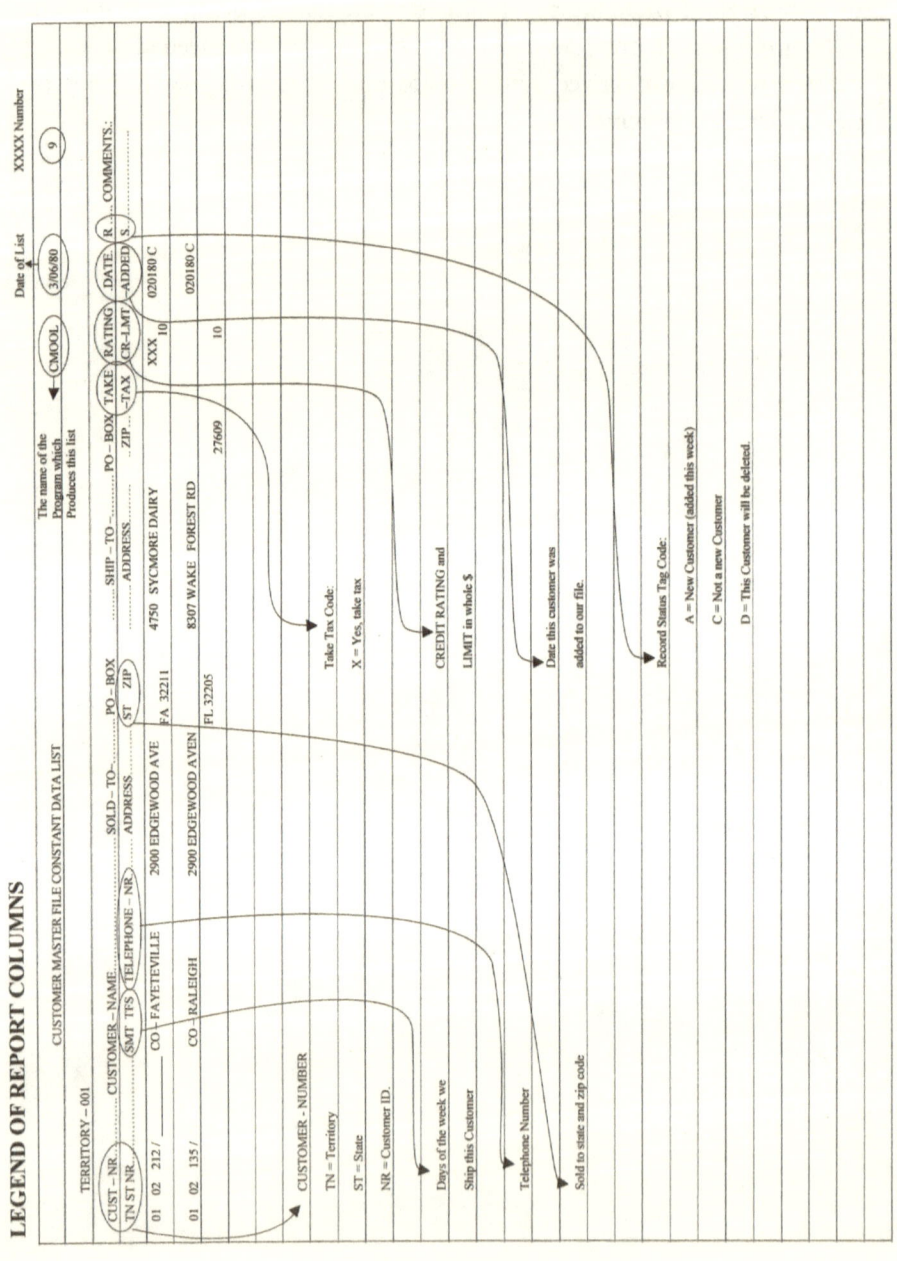

VI

REQUIREMENTS TO CONVERT TO COMPUTERIZED ACCOUNTS RECEIVABLE CREDIT SYSTEMS

The degree of effectiveness of a new computerized Accounts Receivable/ Credit System to the user functions is determined by the amount of planning and preparation that is exerted in the initial stages of implementation. This basic tenet will hold true for the Accounts Receivable system to the credit function, as well as any other system to be converted to a computer.

Planning and preparation for the Accounts Receivable system must begin with the Accounts Receivable/Credit Department with the definition of what an effective accounts receivable system must accomplish for the credit function. Primarily, it obviously must provide decision-making data needed to meet or exceed Accounts Receivable/Credit Department objectives.

These objectives should include:

- .. Achieving budgeted receivables turnover
- .. Minimizing bad debts
- .. Approval of all orders

.. Speedy processing of new customer credit applications
.. Minimizing past due balances

A. *Functional Requirements*

There are a number of functions that must be performed in the Accounts Receivable/Credit Department to effectively manage customer accounts and meet objectives. Accordingly, the accounts receivable system must provide a number of data items to be delivered to the decision-maker quickly and conveniently.

Take functions to be satisfied are:

... Manage all receivables; especially marginal accounts
... Customer contact by phone and letter
... Establishing credit guides (lines)
... Automated order approval
... Exchange of trade payment data
... Monitoring check deductions
... Department staffing
... Liaison with sales
... Monitoring branch operations
... Controlling expenses
... Dunning of customers
... Placement for collection
... Customer visitations

B. *Required Data*

The general data required to provide the decision-making tools for achieving the performance of credit functions are:

Customer name (sold to)
Street address
City, State, Zip

Customer account number
Credit guide (line)
Credit rating
Credit code (type of credit to be allowed)
Year account opened
Payment history
Highest credit extended
Collection activity history
NSF (insufficient funds) check history
Telephone number
Name of contact
Code to identify credit assistant
Ship-to identification

There are additional details (data) that must be provided if specific tasks are to be adequately covered. These are listed below:

Open order file (by each location if needed
Amount owed
Age of oldest and undisputed invoice
Special conditions or terms with customers
Allowable standard for slowness of payment
Codes for future dating
Dollar amount of incoming order
Date of order
Amount of sale
Terms of sale
Invoice number
Purchase order number
Codes to identify adjustments
Signal to identify disputes
Manual order approval
Deduction codes
Allowance for follow-up comments
Record of dunning activity

C. *Processing Requirements*

In order to provide the necessary detail to perform credit functions, certain processes are required to produce timely information.

> . . . Cash application on a daily basis with required file updating
> . . . Sales and credits applied and updated on a daily basis
>
> . . . Daily adjustment processing and updating
>
> . . . Separate open order files maintained on a daily basis

The foregoing listings are the result of an attempt to include all detail needed to perform the credit function objectives. It is recognized however, that there may be some omissions as more and more packaged computer software programs become available. For our purposes though, the requirements listed should provide more than adequate detail for the credit administrator's decision-making.

VII

TOOLS TO IMPROVE COLLECTIONS

Where does the collection effort start? Does it begin with acceptance of an order or invoicing of the shipment? Does it start with the aged trial balance of accounts receivable or the first phone call or dunning letter? . . . .

Actually, the collection effort starts in the embryo stages of establishing a customer account. For new accounts, a New Account Credit Application, Exhibit III, will provide all the required data to initiate an in-depth credit investigation. Established accounts should be requested to complete and sign the application in order to meet requirements of the credit file and to assist in justifying increases in the credit guide.

Management policies should be established, if not already in effect, to enforce the requirement for a complete credit application. Missing data, more readily available at the customer source, is difficult and more time consuming to obtain from a credit office. Delays in order approval more than often result.

The information supplied by the field representative or at the time of initial open credit request by the customer is the ideal time to initiate a complete credit investigation through an accurate and concise credit application.

A new account credit application, completed in detail, is the catalyst by which you expedite approval of new orders and continue to build historical credit files for each of your valued customers. It serves as the base on which credit guides are determined and maintained in order to provide smooth order flow over extended periods.

It is not enough for sales to supply the name of a firm with limited or sketchy information and expect to receive instant approval of an initial $2500 or $5000 order. Mathematically, if one could assign a quantitative value to classes of information; the order value divided by information quality will equal the length of time required to approve a specific order.

The initial priority of a first-rate credit department is to develop sufficient information and account monitoring to react swiftly to the needs of sales and the customers serviced by all operations of a company. Whether manually or on a computerized system the detail needed to satisfy this priority must be developed.

A great deal can be accomplished toward the goal by establishing the following files and monitoring controls.

A. *Credit Files*

Establish complete credit files for all customers with available D & B or other trade reports, financial statements (preferably audited), trade references and ration analyses. It is important to note that the contents of the credit file outlined here and in other chapters is not intended to be all inclusive but surely the major components for an effective file.

Credit files oftentimes include additional items which are dictated by the desires of the credit manager. They can include:

Dunning letters
Call record sheets
Pertinent correspondence
Special arrangements and guarantees
Copy of the first check
Copy of the first purchase order
Payment history
Customer's mailing envelope
Customer complaints
Agency collection activity, etc.

Whatever you choose to include in those credit files should be selected for its relationship to the customer and the credit and collection activity. The credit file must remain flexible enough for ease of reference and not be overloaded with duplicate and irrelevant detail.

B. *Past Due Report*

The reporting system must include data that provides more instantaneous indicators of potential problems with an account and to allow for more accurate and timely approval of incoming orders. One extremely valuable report lists all customers who are 31 days or more past due and over $1000. The parameters can be altered to suit particular requirements such as 16 days past due and $500. The limits may be moved up or down to suit a particular customer base and terms of sale. Whichever parameters are chosen, an additional criteria would be to limit the number of customers who fall within the parameters to about fifty or less. This makes follow-up more dynamic and allows better concentration on the problem. After a period of time, the amount of customers appearing on the report will diminish and parameters may be adjusted accordingly.

The report should be prepared at least weekly for immediate action by the credit department. A most successful method of using this data is to phone each customer to request immediate payment. If a remittance is not received within agreed limits, a registered letter in the form of a firm demand is sent to request payment by a set date. If payment or response is not received, a final call is made. Where satisfactory agreement cannot be reached, the customer is placed for collection on a free demand. This allows an additional 10 days or more before any permanent break in relations occurs and future credibility is affected.

C. *Credit Status Report*

A daily Credit Status Report for all customers who have an order in the open order file (the order backlog) or has had monthly sales activity as its criteria should be prepared for the credit department. The report is also utilized by any personnel authorized to approve orders on a daily basis.

Exhibit IV details the format and information to be used to determine credit status reporting. It measures credit line exposure by taking the current and past due amounts owed along with the amounts to be shipped. If these amounts surpass the established credit line, an asterisk or star is placed on the account to indicate excessive exposure. Daily sales, orders and payments are applied to the report to update required status reporting.

If determinations are made that the amount of exposure is excessive, credit management then has the option to hold orders in the open order file or request immediate payment from the customer to reduce exposure. In any event, the credit administrator is provided with the daily information needed to control exposure for each customer. When used in conjunction with the Accounts Receivable Trial Balance the report provides account status for prompt reaction to daily orders.

Once the above tools to ensure collection are implemented, the credit administrator has available a sound framework on which to build an efficient credit function. These tools provide:

1. A firm customer base against which orders can be readily accepted.

2. A method by which exposure can be adjusted as demand changes.

3. Adjustments to customer credit lines without the need to perform extensive research over again and delay further orders.

4. A reduction of (DSO) Pays Sales Outstanding which increases the company's cash flow and maximizes asset utilization.

5. Acknowledgement and shipment processing is expedited . . . . no delays resulting from additional credit investigations.

6. A reduction or elimination of the burden of collection from sales personnel and virtual elimination of follow-up information gathering from the customers.

VIII

FORECASTING COLLECTIONS

To plan for effective collection of the outstanding receivables, the credit executive must develop a cash receipts forecast. At a minimum, the plan should be completed at each month end for the amount of receivables needed to be collected in the next accounting period. As the experience factor becomes more accurate, a weekly collection forecast will also prove beneficial.

A simple method of forecasting your collections is to analyze the history of percent collections on a day-to-day basis. Collections received are entered and accumulated daily and a percent collected is calculated by dividing each cumulative total by the ending receivable balance. At month end, the total percent collected is also recorded. This method should be followed each month to establish a history file model of collection activity. The model month's activity can be applied to a comparable month for estimating expected collections.

For example, if the month of May having twenty work days, no holidays with the last day of the month falling on Friday is comparable to August in composition; than the collection experience for each week in August can be forecasted using May history as the model. If sixty percent of the monies were collected by the first ten days in May; it can logically be assumed that a comparable amount will be collected in August. For the entire month, if 90% of the receivables were collected in May; then it is reasonable to assume that a target of 90% in August can be attained.

As a word of caution; the collection month should be analyzed carefully when selecting the model data. A different number of workdays in a fiscal month, the number and position of holidays, and the tenth of the month occurring on a weekend can affect the collections percentages. Special cash receipts such as payment of a note, tax refunds, dividends, insurance payments on a casualty loss, etc., should be factored out of normal receipts so as not to distort the collection activity attributable to the normal trade receivables.

A second method of forecasting receivables collections—albeit slightly more complicated—is to prepare a matrix based upon the history of your collection cycle. However, like any other forecasting model, analysis of historical collection data must be performed in order to supply the basic data needed to create the matrix.